Living in Flora

Healing through nature & flowers, prose & poetry

Bobbie A. Sala

Copyright © 2024 (Bobbie A. Sala)
All rights reserved worldwide.

Words & design *Bobbie A. Sala*
Cover photography Bobbie A. Sala
Photography Bobbie A. Sala

No part of this publication may be reproduced, shared, stored, or transmitted by any means, electronic, mechanical, photocopy or otherwise, without the prior permission of the author and publisher. Copyright belongs to the author, Bobbie A. Sala and ASPG. For enquiries, please email livinginflora@icloud.com

Inspiring Publishers
P.O. Box 159, Calwell, ACT Australia 2905
Email: publishaspg@gmail.com
http://www.inspiringpublishers.com

 A catalogue record for this book is available from the National Library of Australia

National Library of Australia The Prepublication Data Service

Author: Bobbie A. Sala
Title: Living in Flora
Genre: Poetry

Paperback ISBN: 978-1-923250-53-6

TABLE OF CONTENTS

Prologue 1

Chapter 1. MIL-FLORES, A Thousand Flowers 2

Chapter 2. SEASONS 11

Chapter 3. MUSIC & LYRICS 38

Chapter 4. HOUSE & HOME. Floral Arrangements
             at Home 42

Index 54

References 56

A Special Thank you! 57

About the Author 58

To:

From:

Date:

*Living in Flora is dedicated to my late mother,
Flora Espinas Aytona
who passed away when I was barely 2.*

*'I have lived my life in your loving embrace,
Mommy. Forever and Always.'*

'For Al, who never fails to make me laugh.'
'For Bella, my one love.'

PROLOGUE

Have you ever felt grief? If no, you are lucky and your time has not come. Once in a person's life, he or she will experience grief. I hope you take some inspiration from this book, if and when you get there. All I can say is that there is happiness and joy if you choose to find it.

If you are like me, who has known grief as a child, then you will be walking along these pages with me as I relive the trauma and happiness of my unique childhood. If you have lost a special someone in your life and that person is a significant part of you, then let's keep going; embrace life with a tear in our hearts and a smile on our faces.

My garden is where I find comfort and calm. It is my private oasis and retreat. I have a preferred colour combination in my garden. You will usually find white and different shades of blue flowers. In spring, you will see the pale pinks of crab apple blossoms.

CHAPTER 1

'MIL-FLORES, A thousand flowers'

As a teenager, I would go to Aunt Salome's provincial house and spend summer there. Growing up in the city, you can tell the difference of provincial life. The fresh air, fresh food and slow life captivated me. It was here in Albay that I found my favourite flower, hydrangeas. The prettiest blue in particular. Something about it made me think about my mother. It's utter beauty and charm without the heavy scent. Unassumingly plain but ethereally big, bold and beautiful. As I sat at Nana Ome's garden steps, staring at these beauties, I ask her with excitement, 'what are those blue clusters of tiny flowers, Nana?' She replies with a smile, 'Mil-flores'.

I sighed heavily. 'Ahhh! Mil-flores! Thousands of flowers! My mommy is sending me her love a thousand times.' I would always ask my aunt for some cut hydrangeas and bring them to the cemetery on a Sunday to visit my mother every summer vacation.

I lost my mother at the young age of two, just a baby. I never knew the cause of her sickness. Nobody ever told me. This happened in the 70s when cancer was taboo. I grew up hearing older people around me hush when they saw me. Family friends, relatives, they would say, 'oh, Baby Bellet, you're so beautiful like your mother … pobresita.' Poor little thing. Their sentences always end with that 'poor little thing'.

When you are a child, you go with the flow and that becomes your normal. My father never re-married. Perhaps it was all my fault. I remember being six or seven. A much older cousin was teasing me, that an American widow was after my dad. My father resembled Robert De Niro when he was young. My cousins called him, our handsome abuelo (grandfather). So, cousin Sally said Dad will go with her to America and leave me behind. I would cry a lot on the floor. Then, he would tell me, 'no, no, Bebe. That is not true.'

As an adult, I'm reminded of those tantrums and selfish, childish behaviours. I watched my father, alone, all these years. He watched me and let me live. I saw his sorrow and pain camouflaged by the handsome smile he always gave me. 'It's all my fault,' I said to myself. 'It's all my fault that he never married. He will be single until the day he dies.'

'Daddy, why did you not re-marry?' He smiled. He never answered these questions.

'What did my mommy die of?'

'Is it C?' His smile weakens and he looks away. 'Please, Daddy, tell me!' The squeal is almost a squawk. 'Is it? Is it? Is it breast, liver … ? Please, Daddy.'

'Stomach.' I heard him say faintly. Afterwards he changed the subject. That was the last time we talked about my mother. Life went on.

Hydrangea macrophylla

Mophead hydrangeas, cultivars of *Hydrangea macrophylla*, are the most commonly grown hydrangeas in our gardens. Mopheads have full, round heads with large petals. Plants are typically rounded with mid-green leaves, and the flowers are either pink or blue, depending on the soil type – if you have acidic soil there will be more lilac flowers, while alkaline soil generates pink blooms.

My very first hydrangea flower bed, Nov 2019

Grow *Hydrangea macrophylla* in moist but well-drained soil in full sun to partial shade. Shelter from cold, drying winds. To promote fresh, new, vigorous growth on established plants, cut back hard in early spring. Prune out one-third to one-quarter of last year's growth to the base each year to encourage the plant to produce new shoots.

The first five years are the formative years and it has the biggest impact on a child's life. Maria Montessori called this the 'absorbent mind'. She compared a child's brain to a sponge, where it absorbs everything. As I think about these important developmental years, two people come to mind. First, my biological mother who is in heaven looking down at me at all times, and my loving aunt, who became my surrogate mother. I grew up calling her Mama. She was the one who guided me through life and taught me how to have a steadfast faith in God. It is through her that I appreciated tailored clothes, potted plants and compact gardens. These are the two women, coincidentally related, for they are first cousins, who were my strength and pillars as I grew into a young, and now mature, woman.

Milestones came and left and they were mostly happy, sometimes tumultuous but momentous!

But there were those times when it was hard. As one grows up, one goes through life's challenges, life's changes, pre-puberty, adolescence, graduation, careers. Friendships flourished, family and friends moved places, loved ones getting married and moving houses. First dates, relationships, first heartbreak, first love etc. One thing I can say is, 'it is just harder to experience life without a mother.' During these formative years, I sought solace over reading, writing, poetry and music. In high school, I won a poem competition. I barely recognised my alias when the winner was announced because it was pronounced differently by a teacher whom I respected. A friend had to nudge my shoulder so I could get up and walk to the stage.

I wish I had kept that winning piece. I didn't.

I had a book of poems I wrote in my teen years. It was a journal. Because I have moved many places and lived in a couple of countries, I have lost them too.

I will try to remember some of them. I guess when you are the writer. You don't forget.

AFTER THE RAIN, 1988

After the rain,

Feeling lost.

Love the love you gave me.

After the rain,

Feeling cold,

Love the warmth you gave me.

After the rain,

Feeling high,

That's just the way your love is lifting me.

© *Bobbie A. Sala Manila, PHI.*

Parterre of Japanese boxwoods (buxus) and white hydrangeas (Agnes Pavelli) in the front yard.

I never knew that a formal garden, big or small, could bring me so much joy. Here in Australia, we have a lot of evergreen shrubs and trees so we don't really call this season, 'fall'. However, there are also a lot of deciduous trees and plants that are always so nice to look at.

Autumn is always a kaleidoscope of colours. The shades of green, blue, purple, yellow, orange, red. Have you ever watched the trees when the seasons are changing? It is always magical. The gradual change from summer to early autumn before the leaves fall. The little pop of green leaves in spring. The tulips, jonquils and daffodils blooming in early spring. The jacarandas filling up the Sydney streets in summertime. Camellias showing off the soft, cashmere petals of magenta, pink and white.

Next time you go for a walk, look around you and see what type of flora there is in your area. Are you the kind who loves scented flowers and shrubs, or do you prefer just looking at the greens? When you look outside and hear the wildlife, the sound of the birds and cicadas, you can't help but feel at peace with nature. Do you have an ache or a longing when you hear the sounds of nature?

Oftentimes, I can hear my mother speak to me. Sometimes without words, just that nice warm breeze wrapping my whole body and that loving feeling. It never goes away. She's never far away.

CHAPTER 2

SEASONS

The beauty of living in Australia is that we have four seasons. I appreciate and look forward to what the garden has to offer each time a new season begins. I have learned the growth cycle of the local plants and flowers that are in season.

Tulips at The Floriade Tulip Festival in Canberra, NSW.

'The beautiful spring came; and when Nature resumes her loveliness, the human soul is apt to revive also.' —Harriet Ann Jacobs

SPRING.

Let us start with my first favourite season: spring. My top three spring flowers and shrubs that I love to grow in the garden. Tulips, daffodils and their varieties and of course, hydrangeas.

TULIPS. Have you ever grown tulips? I started growing tulips a couple of years ago after being inspired by the well-known Danish master gardener, Claus Dalby. Most of his books are in Danish but he released an English version called *Containers in The Garden* which I bought as soon as it was released. He has an Instagram and YouTube channel. I find momentous joy when I watch an episode of him walking in his garden in Denmark and talking about the trees and plants that are growing there, which he planted from seeds, bulbs and/or cuttings – not to mention his charismatic and wholesome humour. Perhaps one day he will open this to the public and I can catch a glimpse of his beautiful creation. I once told him he reminded me of my Papa. He still does!

Dalby has fifteen garden rooms and my most favourite part is the sunken garden. What's not to love?! It is a bevy of beautiful white flowers and green foliage.

While Mr. Dalby has fifteen garden rooms, my ordinary self has two, which by the way, I am so grateful for. The first connects to our outdoor patio and is more formal with boxwood and lilly pilly hedges. I plant petunias on the garden bed during summer and violas and primroses in winter. I think we have the best weather here in Sydney because our winters are mild. We get frost but that's about it. That means we have evergreens and our gardens are never bare.

The Sunken Garden, one of Claus Dalby's fifteen garden rooms in Denmark.

In Australia, we start planting tulip bulbs in autumn which is May, around Mother's Day. Isn't that a fitting time for my thirsty soul? I usually plant white tulips. I have planted black, dark purple and pink ones before.

White tulips in the Laundry Room.

My very first tulip bloom was grown in 2017. I love how this hybrid tulip closes at night as if its petals are in prayers, and open up in the daytime when the sun comes out. This is a shot I took from the laundry room against the white wall. You can see the sun flickering through. In a melancholic mood, these beautiful tulips soothe my soul, and again, bring me closer to my mother.

'My emotions are up and down, open and shut, high and low. Just like a cacharel tulip, I burst with happiness under the sun, open up life's sweetness and joy and some nights, I close and fold like a scared child, scarred at night when the monsters come.' —Bobbie A. Sala

Homegrown tulips planted in containers and pots over the years.

I also have a small sunken garden which I lovingly call 'the laundry garden'. It is located outside the laundry room.

The Laundry Garden.

'We might think we are nurturing our garden, but of course it's our garden that is really nurturing us.'
—Jenny Uglow.

DAFFODILS. If there is anything I love about daffodils, it is their sweet-smelling scent. There is hardly any effort; very low maintenance to grow them. You plant them as bulbs, set and forget! In early spring, the sweet-smelling scent greets me as I open the back door to the laundry garden. I grow all my spring bulbs in pots. They are simple and effective.

White daffodils in the laundry garden.

'To ease another's heartache, is to forget one's own.'
—Abraham Lincoln

Every year, I donate to non-profit organisations like Cancer Council's Daffodil Day. Daffodil Day is celebrated across all the states of Australia around August, early spring.

To Cancer Council, and those affected by cancer, the daffodil represents hope for a cancer-free future. Cancer Council has funded lifesaving breakthroughs in cancer research over the years. By supporting Daffodil Day, we can give hope for a future where all cancer is treatable by funding lifesaving cancer research.

I have supported this not-for-profit organisation for many years as I know how much support they provide to the patients as well as their families. There are so many other not-for-profit organisations anyone can support. What appeals to you and the ones closest to your heart should be the one to guide you.

Tulips, jonquils and daffodils at the Floriade Tulip Festival

SUMMER.

Late nights, early mornings, the beach, the pool. Jasmines and gardenias. Cherries and berries, plums and nectarines, crickets and Christmas beetles. Summer is that special season when family memories are made!

Summer is truly a feeling!

Why do a lot of people look forward to summer? Why do people plan summer vacations and summer holidays? Is it because the sun makes one happy? Yes, I believe so. Just like the stars at night, the sun does not only make one happy but it makes your spirit and body alive. Do you ever wonder why people follow the sunshine when it's cold? Because it heals. It also covers up the heartaches that one can feel. It is a temporary remedy like a cod elixir. Have you ever fallen asleep on the beach under the sun on a sunny summer afternoon? If not, try it. You wake up a completely different, mostly happy, person. Summer sunshine brings smiles, laughter and a whole dose of vitamin D. The summers I mostly remember are the ones that changed my life: falling in love, or getting married, or having a baby or finishing school. It seems that every milestone of my life happened in summer.

Viburnums at home in summer.

Evergreen hydrangeas bloom from spring to late summer.

When we renovated our front landscape, I made sure to put a parterre outside my daughter's bedroom. I want her to wake up each morning looking at the beautiful blue and white flowers amongst the big and beautiful green foliage and hedges. It has been a dream to design and build this garden. One or two years later, this garden is alive with blue and white hydrangeas in the summer and an evergreen foliage all year long.

If you are trying to establish a hydrangea garden and you don't want your garden to look bare in winter, evergreen hydrangeas are something you can consider. They retain their leaves all year long. Evergreen hydrangeas – *Dichroa versicolor* – have flowers that are more compact. They start with white buds and turn blue for a good period of time. Their colours are not controlled by the type of soil. If you have an acidic or alkaline soil, evergreen hydrangeas will always be blue. It's also hardy and low maintenance, making it perfect for anyone who doesn't want to spend hours tending to their plants.

Aside from hydrangeas, my favourite summer flowers are dahlias, crab apple blossoms, cherry blossoms, white lillies, viburnums and star jasmines.

DAHLIAS. There are so many different types of dahlias. Like roses, they have so many varieties and cultivars. I particularly love the 'café au laits', 'dinner plates' and 'cactus' dahlias. Dahlias grow from tubers. The dahlia tubers are easier to plant and do not have a specific planting time compared to tulips. I do like planting them in early summer. When I do, the flowers bloom in three to four weeks' time. I once planted 'café au lait' tubers in December then we went to Europe, four weeks later, I come home with nice foliage and it didn't take long until it had buds. Isn't it amazing how planting and blooming takes time? It reminds me of the line in my favourite book, *The Little Prince,* when the fox said to the little boy, 'It is the time spent with your rose that makes your rose so important.'

Anything that you value, you make time for. Anything that you want to grow abundantly and successfully takes time, attention and care.

A masterpiece is not created overnight.

'It is only with the heart that one can see right. What is essential is invisible to the eye.' —Antoine de Saint Exupéry.

From tuber to flower. 'Cactus' Dahlias

PEONY. Every November, as soon as the jacarandas fill Sydney streets with purple wonder, the pretty peonies come out. In fact, they come out the week of my daughter's birthday, 11th November. Peonies or peony roses are actually native to Asia, Europe and North America. There are so many species and varieties of this flower. Peonies come out late spring and/or early summer. These flowers have a short blooming season, usually only seven to ten days. Peonies like sunny but cooler climates, so there are a lot of peony farms in Victoria. In NSW, there are peony farms in Armidale or in the Southern Highlands. I love white peonies but the pale pink peonies are my favourite because they are my daughter's birthday flowers.

White peonies

A long-stemmed pink peony for each teen who attended my daughter's sweet sixteenth birthday party.

AUTUMN.

Autumn in Australia is very different if one compares it to autumn in Canada. I remember visiting Vancouver in autumn and we went to the mall. My cousin was telling me that I may get cold because I was wearing a skirt and a top with a wool cardigan. This accidental Australian who thinks she can brave the North American cold, said, 'I'll be alright."

That was the last time I wore a skirt on that trip. The cold breeze hurt my legs and my face as I grimaced walking out of the car and back. My cousin had no words, he just laughed at me.

Next to spring, autumn is my favourite season. It is also a coincidence that I am writing this page in May. But more so, it is also a sweet coincidence that May is autumn in Australia and May is of course, Mother's Day.

My mother was named Flora. Spanish for flowers! Flowers of May. Mi Flores de Mayo. My flowers of May.

Bittersweet, it is. Like rubbing salt into the wound. Growing up, at school, Mother's Day and all other days of celebration are major events. I would write a letter to my mother each Mother's Day and I would bring the card home and show it to my aunt, she then told me to place it in the altar, next to the Sto. Niño, (Saint Baby Jesus). There was a time I did this, one afternoon after school, and as I was placing the card on the altar, there was a gentle summer breeze and a tiny whisper calling my name. I ran screaming downstairs and told my aunt. We ended up laughing.

The colour of maple leaves in front of our home turning from green to yellow, then red to brown, eventually losing its leaves to hibernate in winter. How reassuring to think there is a sense of hope in this change of season but only for those who are willing to wait.

Sydney's Hills District in autumn

FALLEN, 2018

Leaves have Fallen

    Souls have risen

Lifeless colours

    Remaining

Cuddling greens

    Comforting

Fallen Loved Ones

    Are just the same

Coloured patriots

    Of beloved name

Tombstone laden

    With greens comfortin'

Honour and praise them

    Come Remembrance Day

© *Florante M. Aytona Vancouver, CA*

CAMELLIAS. Winter rose. I discovered camellias when I moved to this house, that I am still living at to this day. The front lawn was filled with camellia topiary trees left right and centre. My neighbour next door had a lot of those trees too. I was so curious about them as they showcase beautiful blooms each year. They are so lush and abundant that the petals cover the ground. Almost magical. We have two types of camellias: *Camellia sasanqua* (the flower that Coco Chanel made famous!) and *Camellia japonica*. Camellias have such sweet, delicate scent – never overpowering.

Camellias blooming in autumn

Camellias are not the ideal cut flowers, as they exude their beauty on the trees. They are so delicate that the wind can make the flowers fall off. However, I cut the foliage with the flowers. Camellias have beautiful green foliage that I use in the interior of my home. I have seen a lot of camellia foliage that is artificial in home stores. It is humbling to know that I can have fresh foliage all year through.

Fresh cut foliage from the garden

WINTER.

I love winter in Australia! It is cold, frosty and freezing but that's all. I call our winter mild when I compare it to winter in New York and London. In January 2023, we were in London and I loved it because it didn't snow – well, not in the CBD. It almost felt like winter in Sydney. Perhaps climate change is to blame. We have had very extreme weather in the last ten years.

It doesn't snow in Sydney but it does in the mountains and in the Southern Highlands. Friends from overseas get surprised when I say we do have ski resorts here in NSW.

So, not having snow in Sydney, and most parts of Australia, is quite good for the gardens because we have beautiful flowering shrubs all throughout winter.

The flowers and shrubs that grow in winter here are: cyclamen, pansies, violas, primroses, hellebores, chrysanthemums and daisies!

'We need to go through winter so that we can anticipate spring.' —Bobbie A. Sala

CYCLAMENS. Sweet-smelling white cyclamens are my go-to for a pick-me-up in winter. I love placing them in a chinoiserie pot at the foyer, or even at the front porch. Their smell makes you forget the cold. They grow from tubers and are valued for their flowers with upswept petals and variably patterned leaves.

Cyclamens are an interior designer's favourite. You will see them in a small or medium size vase on top of a coffee table or bedside. Kitchen bench top or dining room table. In fact, if you place them anywhere inside the house, or even in a covered patio, they will survive and will give you the sweetest smell there is. Cyclamen have a tuber, from which the leaves, flowers and roots grow. In most species, leaves come up in autumn, grow through the winter and then die in spring. It then becomes dormant through the summer.

Sweet-smelling white cyclamens in winter.

VIOLAS. Ah, Violas, they are like the petunias of winter. If you are familiar with violas, you would understand when I say that they are like little clowns. Sometimes if you look closely, you will find one that actually smiles back at you. They are small ground cover plants with green heart-shaped leaves. Violas are hardy so they can withstand winter frost.

Violas have a delightful sweet scent. I like them in planters and chinoiserie pots and also add them as an accent garden bed on a large topiary planter. Aside from its pretty flowers, it is also considered a medicinal herb and a culinary ingredient. Next time you order your brunch, check out the herbs and flowers on top of your eggs, bread or salad, it will likely be a viola. These flowers are rich in Vitamin A and C.

Pretty violas in winter.

MAGNOLIAS.

Oh, my Magnolias! You know spring is coming when the sweet pink magnolias start blooming. Magnolia trees give a display of colours late winter and early spring. They last for many weeks and driving in a street full of magnolias brings me so much joy. They come in pink, white and magenta colours. All across New South Wales and Victoria, you will see the pink magnolias in spring. I planted my own magnolias in my front yard as a hedge. I picked the 'teddy bear' magnolias for the beautiful teddy bear like foliage. Their leaves are more rounded compared to the 'little gems' which are elongated with pointy tips. The flowers are the creamiest of whites and a light, musky scent. Magnolias are generally considered ornamental trees, but they can also be used and shaped into a hedge. It has an elegance and simplicity to it.

Cut pink magnolias to welcome spring at home.

CHAPTER 3

MUSIC & LYRICS

What would life be without music? Music for me is medicine. Music was my companion when I was scared. Music was my make-believe when I wanted to escape this world's madness. Music is my therapy. Music is my prose and poetry. Music took me places I have never been. Music goes deep – so deep it throbs.

Someone wrote me a song when I was in college.
It goes like this…
'Sometimes late at night you say you love me, Well I guess it doesn't matter very much at all Blah, Blah, blah, blah, And I wonder did I put you there to watch you fall? Did you ever love me at all?'

I barely remember the lyrics but I remember the tune. That person gave me a live recording of it. I can sing these lines today and only myself and that writer will know and understand or remember it. A memory that was once special for a short period of time.

I am very much influenced by Baroque and Classical music. Antonio Vivaldi, Johann Sebastian Bach and George Handel. Their composition draws me in and it brings me healing. I play Classical music when I am anxious. Despite being a frequent traveller, I still get anxious about it and I manage this by playing Classical music on my Air Pods before take-off and before landing. It calms my neurons and my head.

Piano, violin, wind instruments penetrate into my brain like soft bedsheets. It's Classical music for healing. When I broke off a six-year relationship decades ago, I played lots of Classical music and Jim Chappel's *Nightsongs and Lullaby* was on repeat for weeks. It somehow eased my heart and mind even if I cried myself to sleep.

My genre ranges from classical to pop, R&B to jazz, to new age to dance. I really am a sucker for artists who are not in the mainstream. I am attracted to songs that didn't make it to the top 40 but are so deep and powerful that I play their music repeatedly.

Jim Chappell is still very much alive and perhaps the age of my father-in-law now but I was such a big fan of his music in the 90s.

James Taylor is another musical legend. I just missed his concert in Bowral last week but 'Your Smiling Face' and 'If I keep my heart out of sight' are my favourite songs to listen to.

The legendary Tony Bennet greatly influenced me growing up with his old music. There is a certain mood when one plays a certain era of music. Tony outlasted many, many decades.

My dad loved Frank Sinatra and I would hear him play his music during those times when he thought I wasn't listening. Many moons ago, him and his brother would talk about Sinatra as if he was their mate. I may have picked up this Sinatra appreciation blood. When the album, *DUETS* came out in the 90s, I was the first to purchase a cassette tape back then, CD-ROM afterwards and now in this era, I have them in my Playlist.

I truly wonder how the world would be without music. Music is everywhere. It is in nature. It is white noise. It is the river that flows, the flutter of a wren's wings, the sound of raindrops on your window, your mother's soothing caresses, her voice ... those I never had the pleasure of and have always dreamt of having. Somewhere in my dreams, I do hear her. She cradles me and rock me to sleep. She watched me when I had minor surgeries. She was there when I gave birth to my baby girl. I know because I called out her name in the delivery theatre. The midwife told me, 'keep pushing, darling, your mother is not here.' I called for her. I call her in my anguish, in my pain, in my sorrow. She protects me from harm, in a way that is quite complex to explain but those who share the same predicament with me would know. My mother is never not far! She is always here with me.

How did other types of music help me in my moments of despair? I sang! I sang in the shower, in my bedroom, in the bathroom. Becoming a Glee Club member was an experience that kept me out of boredom. I sang in the choir. It was an outlet. I was a soprano. The higher the voice, the closer to heaven.

'Music was my refuge. I could crawl into the space between the notes and curl my back to loneliness.'
—Maya Angelou

CHAPTER 4

HOUSE & HOME
Floral Arrangements Curated at Home

How do you make a house into a home? I think the answer to this is individual and personal. They say a house can only be a home when 'real love' is there.

Having seen and been exposed to different families, relationships, diversities and cultures, I feel very lucky to have grown up in, what I would say, was a pretty ordinary but very nurturing and loving family. A loving husband and a supportive wife. Their children all turned out to be professionals and high achievers. Their love story is unique and one that everyone holds high regard for. Unfortunately, there are some others who did not get this kind of upbringing.

There is a profound psychological effect when a child is a victim of an abusive home. I have heard stories from friends about their own hard experiences growing up. Their stories are those that you see in the movies. Fiction. But hey, they are true stories. I have seen generational trauma passed on and carried out by children unaware that it is real and they are living the nightmare. Psychologically, it destroyed them. Emotionally, it is a struggle. Some have a hard time forging relationships with others due to a lack of self-esteem, or a fear of rejection. There is so much hurt and pain while they are all still alive. How do they live a normal life? How do they negate this emotional trauma they have lived with in their first twenty to thirty years?

Sometimes I ask, which pain is harder? The pain of losing a loved one or the pain of having a loved one who treats you wrong? Which one would you rather have?

Whatever way you answered this question, you can heal. We all can.

One can heal if they choose to. You have to have conviction and eliminate or alleviate the pain. And where do I start healing? When do I stop hurting?

You start healing when you accept the truth. Acceptance, awareness and acknowledgement that your loved one is not coming back. Grieve if you haven't. Take time to grieve. Forgive and move forward.

Easter Sunday at home

HOME IS WHERE THE HEART IS. The first time I lived on my own was when I was awarded a scholarship in Singapore. We had a 3-bedroom flat. I shared my room with another student. Her name was Lilibeth. Lilibeth and I decorated our room like normal twenty-year-old students. We always had a glass vase and would take turns buying fresh flowers on the way home from school. We loved fresh flowers in our apartment. Lilibeth bought all the colourful bouquets while I always bought the white and green ones. She said, 'you're classy.' I said, 'I'm healing.'

After settling down, our first home was an English townhouse in Sydney. I loved filling the house with white lillies, eucalyptus and of course, traditional roses. We planted white geraniums and Mexican agaves and white star jasmines; a pretty landscape in our small courtyard. They bloomed beautifully and continuously all year round.

A few years later, we moved to a free-standing house with two garden rooms and a decent sized front yard. Here, we were able to create the garden of my dreams: a formal garden in the front yard with English buxus (boxwood) hedges and parterre with blue and white hydrangeas. Crab apple trees strategically positioned on the kerbside which gives nice blossoms in spring. Magnolias as a border and a topiary camellia tree as a side gate feature.

The laundry garden is a small courtyard with conifers in planters and landscape grass with star jasmines on the wall. In summertime, the smell of jasmines lingers all through the night.

Another formal garden in the small grass area surrounded with nothing but buxus and lilly pilly hedges. Viburnum and photinia hedges, tall like buildings, surround the pool area and under those are my treasured blue hydrangeas.

The author's friend cutting hydrangeas for her to bring home.

Hydrangeas in summertime.

As a morning person, I embrace the stillness and quiet of dawn. Having a quiet cup of tea watching the sunrise recharges me. These are the times I feel spiritual and these are also the times that I feel closer to my mother.

Sunsets bring me solace in the sense that it is restorative. Sunsets puts me in a sombre, prayerful mood. When you gaze into the horizon and watch the sunset, you can't help but think about how we really are connected to the earth and that we are all mortals. That life here on earth is temporary. And so, we must live it with compassion and dignity, love unconditionally and believe in the power of the divine high.

Freshly picked from the front garden.

Christmas Day at home.

Summer blooms adorn the long table at my daughter's high tea at her 13th birthday.

Camellias from the front garden.

Carnation and erlicheers in spring

'Given enough time and distance, the heart will always heal.' —Laura Fitzgerald

INDEX

-A-
After the Rain 8
Autumn 10,28,29
Acceptance 44
About the Author 58
Awareness 44
Acknowledgement 44
Antoine de Saint Exupéry 24

-B-
Baroque music 39
Boxwood 9,45
Birthday 26,27,50
Buxus 9,45

-C-
Cancer Council
Crab apple tree 1
Claus Dalby 12
Containers in the Garden 12
Camellias 31,32
Cyclamens 34
Carnation 52
Classical music 39

-D-
Daffodils 17
Daffodil Day 18
Dahlias 24,25
Dreams 41

-E-
Erlicheers 52

-F-
Flora 28
Fallen 30
Frank Sinatra 40
Floral Arrangements 42

-G-
Garden rooms 12

-H-
Hydrangeas 4,5,7,9,22,46,47,48,49
Healing 44,45,53
Home 43,45

-J-
Jim Chappell 40
James Taylor 40

-L-
Laundry garden 16,17
Loneliness 41

-M-
Montessori 6
Mothers Day 14
Magnolias 36,37
Music 4,38

-P-
Pain 43
Parterre 9
Peony 26,27
Psychology 43

-S-
Spring 12
Sunken Garden 13,16
Summer 20,21,47
Sunset 48

-T-
Tulip 11,12,14,15,19
Tulip Festival 11
The Little Prince 24
Trauma 43

-V-
Violas 35

-W-
Winter 33

REFERENCES

Dalby, Claus. 2020. Containers in Garden. Aarhus, Denmark
Gardeners World. https://www.gardenersworld.com
House and Garden. houseandgarden.co.uk
Cancer Council NSW. cancer.org.au

A SPECIAL THANK YOU

To Mr. Claus Dalby, for allowing me to feature the Sunken Garden amongst his garden rooms in Denmark.

ABOUT THE AUTHOR

Bobbie A. Sala

Bobbie lives in Sydney, Australia with her husband and daughter. She has one spoiled Frenchie named Bruno.

www.ingramcontent.com/pod-product-compliance
Lightning Source LLC
Chambersburg PA
CBHW041150110526
44590CB00027B/4187